My Book about Church

CONCORDIA PUBLISHING HOUSE • SAINT LOUIS

Dear Parents,

Reading with your child gives you both wonderful gifts. It instills a love for reading and learning. It teaches about the world and its people, increases language skills, and improves vocabulary. You connect on an intimate level, and it's fun.

Use this book as a tool to introduce your child to Jesus, the Savior we all need. Born in sin that separates us from our holy God, we cannot stop sinning. To save us in His great love, God gave His only Son to die to take the punishment for our sins. Jesus rose from the dead and claimed victory over sin, death, and the devil. Those who believe in Jesus receive the gifts of forgiveness of sins and a new life, now and forever.

Young children may not be ready to hear all the words or look at all the pictures in this book. Read as much as they'll allow, use your own words, or simply look at the pictures. Tell your child that you love and care for him or her and so does God. Ask your child to repeat a word or phrase or point at something on a page.

As attention span grows, read more words. Children love repetition, so read this book again and again. As your child grows, ask him or her to tell about the pictures or pause to let him or her finish words or phrases.

Include reading and prayers in your nighttime routine. Teach your child to pray by folding hands, closing eyes, and saying a simple prayer, such as, "Dear Jesus, thank You for loving me. Amen." Ask your child to finish prayers, such as, "Dear Jesus, thank You for . . ." Thank God for family members and friends and pray for their needs. Pray before meals, asking children to copy your words and actions. As your child grows, teach the Lord's Prayer by repeating phrases.

God loves you and your child. May He bless you as He partners with you to raise your child in the love, mercy, and joy of Christ, our Lord.

This edition published 2023 Concordia Publishing House
3558 S. Jefferson Ave., St. Louis, MO 63118-3968

1-800-325-3040 • cph.org

Copyright © 2019 Concordia Publishing House

Written by Cynthia A. Wheeler
Illustrated by Kathy Mitter

Manufactured in Effingham, IL/036670/340964

We go to church to
hear God's Word.

We learn about the Bible, God's love, and Jesus.

We see other members of God's family.

Our pastor leads us to worship God.

We confess our sins and receive forgiveness for Jesus' sake.

We sing songs of praise to God.

Sometimes a choir sings too.

We hear God's Word from the Bible.

Our pastor preaches God's Word.

We participate in Baptisms.

We receive God's gifts and blessings
in Holy Communion.

We pray to God together. He hears
and answers us.

Our pastor cares for us.
We care for him too.

At home, we keep learning about Jesus.